Something Impossible Happens

Something Impossible Happens
©2014, M.K.Sukach
ISBN: 9781937806040
Big Wonderful Press, LLC
Brooklyn, NY

Cover Art ©Tomasz Walenta/marlenaagency.com
Design by Big Wonderful Press

All Rights Reserved.

Acknowledgments
"Family Photo." *Connotation Press.* 2013.
"Mother Tongues." *Quiddity International Literary Journal and Public-Radio Program.* 2013.
"History of Dinosaurs." *Construction Magazine.* 2013.
"Unintended Metaphors." *Yamassee.* Print. 2013.
"War Story." *War, Literature, and the Arts.* 2013.
"Impressions of Light." *The Sim Review.* 2013.
"Bird Box." *JMWW.* 2013.
"Love Story: a Rough Chronology." *Overpass Books.* 2013.
"Professor." *The Laughing Dog.* Print. 2013.
"I Think I Think About of Billy Collins." *Subsynchronous Press.* 2013.
"Invocation." *Sow's Ear Poetry Review.* Print. 2013.
"Ingenuity." *Redactions: Poetry, Poetics, & Prose.* Print. 2013.
"Neighbors." *The Hamilton Stone Review.* 2013.
"Restoration of Breakwater Bridge." *The Blast Furnace*, Volume 2, Issue 3. 2012

Table of Contents

Epigraph	5
Mother Tongues	7
Professor	8
Restoration of Breakwater Bridge	9
Neighbors	11
Family Photo	11
Invocation	12
Quantum Entanglement	14
Bird Box	15
Love Story: a Rough Chronology	17
Unintended Metaphors	18
Ingenuity	19
Stalled	20
War Story	21
A Found Pastoral	22
"Just the Two of Us"	23
I Think I Think about Billy Collins	26
Impressions of Light	27
Oh My God Particle	28
History of Dinosaurs	30
Whisht	31
Existentialism	32
Once in a While	33

Epigraph

For Una Mulligan

I don't ride roller coasters but have tendencies,
swallow hard when a life guard looks away;

four out of five is not a good risk assessment
for love or pain, likeliness or potential for,

and I don't watch the presidential elections
I might lose my heart and mind, bad memories

are fine if you know where they are at all times;
I resist the temptation to revisit old rooms,

and if the house of your childhood was sold,
it's their problem, now, don't say you're sorry;

it's exhausting these worries that's exhausting;
I shy away from any tongue depressor and kiss

back because that's how it's supposed to be;
I've only moved nine times in my life's life:

my hands always ticking away and toward each other
impossible and inevitable, impossible/inevitable;

I have to think about breathing when going off
the rails, the closet door with hooked coats,

a sweaty hand under the sheets at bedtime
taking the pulse from my thigh, the hand

from my hand; in the street I avoid standing
in crowds, look for crossings, and keep a good pace;

pending the forecast, I might like to go outside
even so, I'd need to know if there was a meadow.

Mother Tongues

I heard their English well enough, but burbled
my tumbling lung song of fluid light,

then room light--pallid florescent, a blue
or bluish hue. I hummed blue for some

time until I was made to use a plastic spoon,
the patterns of my vegetable speech, radish...

I spoke radish for weeks, then apple,
and much later, after seashells and fire,

after college, where I mastered a rare garble
of sandy argot, into my house flew a bird

and I picked up wind, chatted tall in tree,
whispered night, prattled bone, and bayed moon.

Professor

For Donald Anderson

I sometimes try to interpret the look on your face,
when you're grading papers in the late afternoon.

Today your hands hover low like barn swallows
over an open book of just discovered poems.

You are saying, I don't have anything to profess
that isn't already written and available for us.

You are saying, I can't eat a whole snowmobile
and that's important if you're a humming bird.

You are saying, I was a soldier for their wars
but what I love now is softer, less ridiculous.

You are saying, I can't help but see wild horses,
dance with my wife, question what's expected.

You are saying, if my obituary is a crossword,
please don't guess, I'd hate to think you remiss.

Restoration of Breakwater Bridge

Always do these rough minded fishermen
cast and sway in their rhythmic persistence;
and the well-oiled girls on elbows perch,
their novelettes dog-eared beside them.

You could, I suppose, imagine Poseidon
in briny robe and conch shell slippers
had just waltzed over the Atlantic;
or conjure a half-sunk and snorting sub
ushered by a fleet of dolphins, who nudge
the sorry hulk like a wounded pup
back to the safety of its amniotic harbor;
or any such cosmic shenanigans.

Knee-deep boys muscle the sea and shore;
they know by now the tides flow both ways;
later they will learn lighthouses welcome
and warn, shipwrecks are treasures, and old
worlds persist in the salt and bone of the fish.

The bridge rulers outward in feet and inches
each year the men leg in further from the edge
of our concaved shore to reach the bay's break-
water island which like myth seems more distant
the closer they get—halfway, then half that.

A buoy bell rings and we end the day;
recover our pails and shovels,
collapsed umbrellas tucked like lances
beneath our arms, and seem bewildered
that not one of us has seen a fluke or a fin.

Perhaps we've stared at the horizon too long,
or wished too hard for our gods to surface,
got tired of waiting and built ways of crossing
the plenum of their world and the vacuum of ours.

By night the workers with reason enough
leave on the lights and their labor undone.

Neighbors

Nothing Harriet ever planted lived.
We profess it's hard not to rejoice in the seed
refused by the earth or, more to the point, her,
bent over the soil she puzzles in all afternoon.
Because that's how she feels about it.

We're charmed by John's metallic gray '67 Shelby
coupe—jilted aviary, blocked, and brooding.
The twin Le Mans stripes speeding over the hood
that now shelter its blown motor and families
of sparky sparrows and pinky mice.

Mary has tried a million times to win
the lottery, leave her husband, and orgasm
by herself on nights when she is left
to revel in all things that don't work.
We love her.

Retired or let go—we think the latter—the Colonel
slogs the post and chats with everyone standing
in slippers and robes by their mailboxes for another notice
of rejected jobs, poems, insurance claims
or, if one of us is lucky, something more formal
listing the lucky one as the primary beneficiary.

We'll have you know no one has bothered
to fill in the thriving potholes mining
our cobbled road with no outlet.
We're all just a little joyful and jealous
of them…of their arrogant and easy labor.

Years from now documentarians might descend on our hovels
to survey the heterotopic site of a people who persisted
in the splintered syntax of the Nation's language,
who transgressed the discursivity of suburbial instantiations,
who lived elapsed and, therefore, preterit lives.

However they say it, they can't do anything more for us...to us the bullets, the bank, and the bottle haven't already done.

Family Photo

If we extrapolate a guess, those are gills
or soft abrasions just below my ears.
Although I appear happy enough, the shock
of the star-white flash must have startled
and pinned open those blood-red wild eyes.
But there I seem to be, the impression of a life
in a goose down elephant-grey winter coat
with homemade mittens stitched to my sleeves.
More like a smirch of disfigured light captured
escaping, a frozen motion warped in the lens,
seated in a hospital room atop a full-body
cast plastered up to hold my father together
after he drunk-crashed mother's third car.
That's her blur standing on the other side
with her head cut off and one hand resting
where my father's twice-broken knee
should be. We were "insolvent" back then.
Those are my used bowling shoes criss-
crossed as if my feet played by themselves.
Disfigured bodies do that kind of thing.
The time father drove us into the river
my mouth opened, but no howl came out.
My fingers clutched to nothing safe.
In the police photo, I'm dog paddling.
It's hard to tell what I'm swimming for,
the raft or the arms or the rope.

Invocation

Imagine Noah thinking he'd never finish on time.
Rushing with hammers, going at the ark
to pound a nail or two by night,
then sitting on one of a forest of stumps
under the creepy stars and cursing in Hebrew.
I mean, I swear not to curse,
but I'm worse than my old man,
who could cuss up a lung for stubbing a toe.

It wasn't as if he had the blueprints for a go-cart,
or even a goat-cart, to build on weekends
for the kids. Hell no, God said, and He spoke in cubits,
He wanted a ship; and far from a lemonade stand
with sails, but something akin to an aircraft carrier.
Because Lord knows he had to get, what,
at least two elephants in there, and in pairs,
as many as earth bred of bugs.

Not to go overboard, but think of them...
the bugs he had to put up and put up with.
There's the bug of throwing up, so two of those.
The bug of pestering. Then the more obscure
Bwg as in ghost or hobgoblin, and imperfections,
bugs that make for shipwreck. Thrown in with
a couple of secret bugs. The zealot's bug
for holy wars, the priest's for altar boys....

So what do you think that pigeon meant,
when after all that rain and dung, Noah stood
at the bow of his cypress freighter and let loose
his holy bird? Depends. I mean, my old man
had two kinds of "Jesus Christ Almighty."
One he wailed while trying to smash up
the air in the kitchen. But one, sometimes,
when he said it, I swear, he was praying,

for what I don't know, but my brother and I
would tiptoe downstairs and just sit beside him.

Quantum Entanglement

After "Anything can happen" by Seamus Heaney

He ate violins
by the dozens
like drumsticks

and if he finished
in the allotted time,
drank himself silly

under the pier
that stretched far
into the sea

over which terns
skipped like flat
stones whose small

ripples swelled and rose
into the notes
of a hurricane

on the other side
of the earth
which, unpawled,

spun a little
while wild
into the cosmos

just shy of beyond a place
where another voice
he swore sang, too.

Bird Box

It is always six O'clock or seven, Sunday
or Monday, October, this year or another
in a bird box with penciled-out holes
through which just enough light passes.

Nothing seems to change between two men talking
without saying anything but understanding everything
until the waitress interrupts what they are not saying
and at least one looks up to say what he'll have.

Everything spins in the street. The black lab, for example,
turning tighter circles directly proportional to the radius
of the leash a woman is desperately trying to correct
by reversing her spin on the ball of her opposing foot.

Can't think about much else when you find a bird
in your living room, which is still unpainted, lamps
and chairs a party huddled together in the center;
and there's the book you lost, or thought you lost.

A bird cradled to your chest will listen to your heart.
The emergency animal clinic nurse understands this.
Try to imagine a quiet way of saying you were amazing.
Think he will be alright? And I want it to be true. Yes.

After a late dinner, a silence during the drive home,
I wanted to say something silly about the two men seated
next to us in the restaurant or the woman pirouetting
with her dog. The bed is where we talk. So, I wait.

You hand me my toothbrush, I pass you the toothpaste. We are married like that. I'm still awake when your bird hand settles on my chest. I can feel your heart beating. Little bird heart, I think. Some hands are expert at this.

Love Story: a Rough Chronology

Falling.
Humming not the love songs per se
but the commercial for Hits of the 70s
packed in a 4-CD box set after our first date.

Ecstasy.
No omens presented themselves and no birds gave sign.
There was no stealing Juliet away and no Westside songs.
Dancing was forbidden and we had to be back by the next moon.

Endurance.
Cherry Blossoms aside, tourists made the festival worth the stroll;
we particularly enjoyed the couple from Texas arguing over the age of trees
and something more uncertain about the South in general.

Rekindling.
"We've reached the glaciers," announced the ship's captain.
So you flopped back on the bed and slung your pants on
and told me to hurry as you stuffed one foot in a shoe
while troubling single-handed with the clasp of your bra.
Our cabin was too small to do things at the same time
so I just leaned a little and loved the whole routine.

Wisdom.
I let the dog out, you let the dog in. I make breakfast,
you sleep till noon. I go to work, you are still at work.
I pass you on the stairs, you hand me our laundry.
You say look, I see. I think, you hear. You're busy, I'm late.
You will, I do. I am, you were. The love is in between.

Unintended Metaphors

    Classical Latin orchis refers to any of various kinds of
    orchid; from ancient Greek ὄρχις, testicle.

First to emerge from the car is not your leg or arm,
groceries you demand I help with or even the dog

but a shivering black-spotted emerald orchid bound
by silver twist ties to a dull garden-green pine dowel.

What surprises me is not the mottled orchideae per se
nor the way my tongue grazes the roof of my mouth

when I mispronounce the Latin I later learn stems
from the Greek, orkhis, but the chagrin at what I bear

in common with this flower you drop on the garage
floor amidst plastic sacs of apples and egg noodles.

Ingenuity

A lever can move the world, a stick a stone.
Birds fashion hooks to fish worms from a pot.

Ford put moonshiners on the road, moon-
shiners stilled moonshine in their Fords.

e.e. cummings made rain in poems rain. The moon
we made just days after launch the year I was born.

My dog will lick and nudge and skate a tinfoil pan
across the floor, then paw it to keep it from budging.

Rosetta's stone now fits in a phone that sits as small
as a little blue bird biting big hard words soft & small.

No wine glass, a coffee cup, no cup, the bottle;
no power, a pen, no ink, a pencil, then blood.

My wife places apples slices on the stone
outcropping that defends this quiet patio

where I read and write and smoke too much.
"So the bears and wolves and crows can eat."

Inshallah, I am still sitting there learning old words
from a book the beasts can already read in the dark.

Stalled

"Of what the world is really made,
we are such easy prey," said Nietzsche.
Black ice, reckless driving, loose dogs
weaving through rigged parking meters
lining the curb like a kickbacked jury.
I kept the bladed key coldly cranking
my morgue-bound German standard-shift,
hoofed my frozen boot at the grudging
pedal, bred the engine down to clicks,
a Gatling gun jammed in a nuclear age.
No spark, fuel, the block bled out black;
pressed to all fours, I nuzzled against the fender
to make sure, crouched above the motor
silent as ice...as if there were a heart to gnaw.

To WWII POW TSgt Hugo Cappelli, 423rd Bomb Squadron, 306 Bombardment Group, 40th Combat Bombardment Wing, 1st Bombardment Division, Thurleigh Airfield, Eight Air Force; Engineer and Top Turret Gunner whose B-17G, "Belle of the Blue," was shot down by German fighters Tuesday, 12 September 1944, at 1128 hours.

War Story

"What used to get me were the guys that been, maybe, once.
And maybe not even in the shit, not forward like us.
They got a thousand pictures of guys they don't know.
They got a rusted rifle and stories about crappy food.
Got a Bronze Star for just being blustery about everything.
Homecomings would really get to me. This one guy was wearing his.
It got caught on his wife's dress and fell into her bra. Priceless.
She jiggled her boobs until it dropped between her legs.
As the guy bent down to pick it up, this hulking ruck slid off
his shoulder and pulled the rest of him to the ground.
The wife turns this beet red and the guy staggers back up
and cracks her right in the mouth. But that wasn't the thing.
It was the guy's two kids suddenly retreating behind the wife,
while he stood fumbling to find the spot for the Star over his heart."

A Found Pastoral

What a marvelous second gesture toward the beautiful
bucolic barns and revelations of wood and bugs in wood;
the poem like a deed to an old claim the critic is banking on;
pain in the bent rough iron of the place; a cobble stone path
teethed in weeds, that once lead to the aspiring gabled roofline
of a cathedral Saltbox, now crumbles off and somehow away
from counter-weighted chains, hay hooks, trochaic rusted / tin can
wind chimes that no longer adorn or sing / but blight and bump
back / a clunky operose apostrophe / to what passes on the road,
the pathos of superb lineation channeling the breath for reading
the line's crestfallen ironic resuscitation of loss and Lacanian foreclosure
presaging the real ruin: no banker / no mortgage / no mortgage
mercy / no souls—a lyrically chiastic recapitulation of negation
and absence; "broken open gates," "splintered rails," "tilted tractor
carcasses," delicately hardened preservations of bankruptcy
Lorded over/ by a token cross rooted in the field / and a conclave
of apostolic crows, who circle the air indifferently, remainders
celebrating nature's long division and decay, what is inevitable;
though there must have been moments, subversions of joy
when the poet's acute focus and measure found insatiable
prospects for "trudging" life: pedantic inchworm / scaling
the spiny rib of a leaf, / has no idea of our century, / nor how
slow is his progress and refrains; for here no one shoots the coyotes
who parse these vestiges of what was always theirs before it was ours;
the house is a bird house, mouse hole, spider web, raccoon rafter,
a cat's cradle the county has long since scheduled for reclamation.

"Just the Two of Us"

Listening to Bill Withers

It was one of those days

when a car crashes,

people die somewhere,

something horrible happens

in Kansas, an aside,

Key West is popular,

again, we've escalated

so they escalate, rape

makes every front page,

porno companies reproduce

front page rape which grosses

millions, one from the four out of five

doesn't make it;

then you walk in and I ask

how was your day, and you say, "Okay"

and I feel safe and loved and hated

and all at the same time, I imagine

Zeno's paradox from the couch

watching the evening anchor narrate

drone strikes in a rectangle box

over his shoulder and think, yeah,

we've had it, and then I lose track

or forget what "it" is because

"it" lacks an antecedent,

like my father's bromidic weather

reports: it's raining, it's hot, it's a tornado,

it's quantum shit happens

...marvelous, I think,

how wonderful and perilous,

I like the world just how *it*

is, the idea that to get to you,

to recognize I need you,

requires I go half way,

then half that, and how small

but up your mouth curves

when you answer

what was that kiss for

just because.

I Think I Think about Billy Collins

When there's not enough left in the bottle
to bother pouring a glass—meaning, you siphon off
what's left by tilting back in the chair, with
everything you have balanced on two legs that aren't yours
but on which you now depend for what remains.

I think I think about Billy Collins and curse
into the clutched body of the bottle
that holds the distilled stink of my breath
and all the inky words that stain and bite
into the glass that whistles by pursing your lips
and blowing where the bloated, lost cork will never fit again.

Impressions of Light

Flashlight is for saving Jim, who would have preferred a kiss
to a dare deep inside a crawlspace infested with rattlesnakes

Spotlight emerges for the missing, the fled, the taken, even the runway
cover girl stoically concealing the pinpricks of sweat in her tiny armpits

Penlight extends like a cigar gritted between the teeth of thieves
and midnight readers—both want in and sometimes don't make it out

Twilight reveals that part of all love is dark and can wait out the tides,
all night long for you to throw up, to balance a bike, to make it across thin ice

Moonlight can be eclipsed with the thumb placed at the proper focal distance;
this is useful to prevent madness, untimely infatuations, and pawing like a cat

Starlight often appears as a decaying arc, the final impression of entropy,
an expended pen's last lost word and yet everyone rejoices when a star falls

Highlight likes to skate around the pages with a seeming insouciant precision
that raises the librarian's ire inversely proportional to the sine of her scowl

Oh My God Particle

Jumping off a bridge...

if jumping off a bridge was everyone's big idea

if my red bike and I were to jump off a bridge (with everyone else)

if I was curious and aloof, serious and glib, thoughtful and reckless

if Jeanie admired my red bike, blue sneakers, in general, my panache

if boys who were extra and blue kissed Jeanie in season across the bridge

if one kiss equals a thousand and Jeanie moved away to college

if by the thousands not one us grew up that well-adjusted

if 4 out of 5 English majors still think bridges are metaphors

if I bought a guitar to lean in a corner and you said it was a symbol of virility

if god 1) makes a puzzle, 2) even he can't solve, 3) solves it, 4) repeats the exercise

if your emotional deficits were displayed as tarot or ornamental lawn gnomes

if later you decide to cross that bridge when you come to it, then got married in Kansas

if the waitress looks only at your wife and you don't like to admit you like that, too

if the number of people either of you slept with is greater
than the sum of both together

if your sex life picks up only in intervals between now and again

if you prefer having dinner next to people who are also alone at the counter

if 1) falling in love 2) with your wife is 3) like a puzzle 4) even you
can't solve

if visiting the public library is not the turn on it used to be

if you could have it to do all over again and this time Jeanie had a sister

if novels are really just the 400 pages of recycled blurb

if your work weeks are becoming a euphoric and blissful descent into aphasia

if we can all finally agree calling it "the God particle" is
metonymically stupid

if you stop shaving for days at a time and those who shave daily
take it personally

if by chance you have a quick question about how to fix all
the broken shit in your life

if the bridge were to collapse, something impossible happened,
and it wasn't a miracle

History of Dinosaurs

The chicken dreams of hot marsh and brackish
pools, how he came to be oppressed or granted
free range as if dominion wasn't his to begin with.

The chicken is full of self-loathing and grieves
at the cruel joy he takes witnessing his kind
collectively squandered and ceded to the will

of the farmer's twisted hands and careless axe.
When there is no work of heads upon the stump,
he imagines a time before man marketed bird meat;

when fowl ruled. Descendants of the great Tyrant
Lizard King, meat eaters! If he could just stomp
the earth, his claws might appear, gnaw the fence,

his teeth might sharpen, evolve into crushing jaws,
his pterodactyl tongue lash at the wounds of his first
kill. But long is the road and hard that out of his coop

would lead to his Jurassic rout. If only he could beat
his wings into cudgels or hands to wring the necks
of uprights crazed in their herbicidal ether dome;

he could preside again in this once jungled earth
thunder his command over this oval office, gaveling
foundations to rubble, ruling us back into the Stone Age.

Whisht

The trees woke and stretched skyward, then,
forgetting themselves, leaned,

thankful for the walkway lamps, who marched on
steady throughout the night in precise feet

per candle, per trunk, per tree. Thus trained not to
expect such gratitude,

a curious sentry paused and peeked out from under
his lid and said, you're welcome.

As the trees bowed lower still to inquire after the
name of this novice light

the paper lady's fire-breathing truck ground its gears
and grumbled over the hill.

The wind rustled up to rouse the birds who signaled
from their nests

tiered above the watch in the branches of the trees,
who shuddered, stood, and held.

Existentialism

Twice I've flipped a beetle right-side up and now

must pass off another decision.

But I pause observing his legs thin

as clock hands juggle time,

his last decisive concession

to despair. I don't know why this irks me.

Something more determined than being fed up

with the animal kingdom, diminishing returns

in a world of cruelties,

one too many irreconcilable

conditions. Aren't interventions all ritual for us?

I thought it was cliché to keep taking it

lying on your back and interrupted.

I wish I had the will to keep righting you,

the decency

to just put down my foot.

Once in a While

It's good to mischief around some mornings

with only the happy go lucky horseplay

of the dog who leaps so often at the bowl

he's taken to hovering ... beside you,

and after that business is settled, the faucets

finally leaking in tune with the fluttering

clock nesting in the rafters above the pot

swinging its feet through the fire, to hear

and feel the rasp of the iron latch lifted,

the wince and creak of Spring's swollen wood

door begrudging the effort but suffering

the push nonetheless to open upon the image

of a prancing fox ... seeming in midair

to notice you not wearing slippers anymore.

www.ingramcontent.com/pod-product-compliance
Lightning Source LLC
Chambersburg PA
CBHW021639080526
44584CB00015BA/1606